Muppet Manners
(Or the Night Gonzo Gave a Party)

STARRING JIM HENSON'S MUPPETS

By Pat Relf • Illustrated by Tom Leigh

Muppet Press/Random House

Copyright © 1981 by Henson Associates, Inc. THE MUPPET SHOW, MUPPET, and MUPPET character names are trademarks of Henson Associates, Inc. All rights reserved under International and Pan-American Copyright Conventions. Published in the United States by Random House, Inc., New York, and simultaneously in Canada by Random House of Canada Limited, Toronto. A Muppet Press Book produced by Henson Organization Publishing in association with Random House, Inc.

Library of Congress Cataloging in Publication Data:
Relf, Pat. Muppet manners (or the night Gonzo gave a party). SUMMARY: The Muppets amusingly demonstrate good etiquette— sometimes by doing the wrong thing.   1. Etiquette for children and youth.   [1. Etiquette]   I. Leigh, Tom.   II. Title
BJ1857.C5R38   395′.122   80-24087   ISBN: 0-394-84713-X   Manufactured in the United States of America   1 2 3 4 5 6 7 8 9 0

So you want to have a party. Well, you've come to the right book. You are probably bursting with questions, just like thousands of other potential party-givers. "What do I do if no one comes?" "What happens to the donkey after his tail is pinned on?" "Who should bring the baloney sandwiches?" "Is it all right to use disposable chairs?" And "How do you spell R.S.V.P.?"

These and many other vital questions are answered in this handy little book. So, read, relax, and enjoy yourself!

Manners

The key to a successful party is *planning*. Your invitations must be tasteful (sardine is always a popular flavor) and should be sent to your guests well ahead of time. If the party is to be a formal affair, let your guests know what to wear by saying "Make sure to wear an undershirt" or "Please paint your feet."

As your party draws near, make sure that your home is spanking clean.
Remember: a place for everything and everything in its place,
and when the place gets too crowded, there's always room
under the bed. (By the way, you might want to
hide that fungus farm of yours in your
sock drawer. It will be safe there.)

Always take particular care in dressing. Your attire sets the tone for
the evening. The perfectly groomed host knows that there's nothing like
a tasteful anchovy bow tie to spice up an otherwise dull evening costume.

Thoughtful guests will bring their
host a small gift, such as rubber
bands or gravel. You will, of course,
want to put the gravel in water
at once. Don't forget to say
"Thank you very much. I just *love*
gravel," even if you prefer mud or
shredded paper.

Hang up your guests' coats neatly, taking special care not to wrinkle or dirty them. If an accident occurs, and you spill purple ink on a guest's coat, remember: salt, flour, concentrated orange juice, and a little more ink will remove the stain.

Proper introductions are essential to
any successful social gathering. Be certain
everyone at your party meets everyone else.

It is correct to introduce a four-headed monster in a clockwise direction, starting with the head closest to you. Upon being introduced yourself, say "How do you do?" and shake hands. Shaking hands with a chicken poses a difficult problem. Our advice is to wing it.

To make your guests feel at home, offer them something to eat before dinner. Prepare the food beforehand to avoid the embarrassment of having to say "Your guess is as good as mine" when a hungry guest asks, "What's there to eat?"

Some of your health-conscious guests may be on diets, so be sure to provide a few special snacks for them, such as slimmers' seaweed and lo-cal olive juice. And do not, under any circumstances, let the words "fatso" and "tubby" slip into your conversation.

Polite conversation is light and inoffensive. As host, you must try to steer the talk toward subjects that will be harmless to even the most sensitive guest.

Certain topics will lead naturally to a pause in the conversation. Since you're obviously not going to cook dinner, this is the time to tactfully suggest leaving for a restaurant.

When taking guests to a restaurant, the host is expected to provide transportation. If traveling by car, help your guests in by opening the door and then carefully setting it aside.

A good driver always thinks first of his passengers' safety and comfort. Remember the hairdos of those in the back seat, and offer to roll up your window.

Choose an elegant restaurant for your guests, one with class,
style, and polish.

To get the best table and especially
good service, slip a fish or two
to the headwaiter. If you're
lucky, you might get a table
near the kitchen.

Do not grab at food across the table. Lasso it. Or, if you have forgotten your rope, say "Please pass the cream of moss fricassee."

Never tuck a napkin into your collar. Instead, place it neatly across your lap. If you don't have a lap, your feet will do.

When eating a meal of several courses, you will be given a set of
utensils for each course. Start with the spoon and fork on the
outside and work your way *in* toward the middle, eating the knife
and butter plate last.

GUESTS: take at least one taste of everything on your plate, no matter how disgusting it is. Moss stew or spaghetti with moss balls may challenge even the strongest stomach; however, it is essential not to offend your host. After all, he has ordered exactly what *he* likes to eat.

It is exceedingly rude to make slurping sounds while eating. The polite diner makes only sloshing, whooshing, and thwak-a-thwak-a noises.

Never place your elbows on the table, no matter how many you have.

Avoid juggling with your mouth full.

And never, but never, sing, whistle, or tap-dance at the table. If it is absolutely necessary, say, "Excuse me," and tap-dance behind your napkin.

A good headwaiter will ask whether you have enjoyed your dinner. It is considered poor form to reply with such terms as "Blecch," "Yucch," or "How long do I have to live?" The proper reply is: "We found the meal quite wretched, thank you." If you want to avoid answering the headwaiter altogether, you are perfectly correct in saying "May I please be excused? I must attend to my ocelot," and leaving the table.

At the end of the meal, the host asks for a bill.
If a Bill seems too large, the host should immediately
send him back and ask for a Stan or a Mike instead.

To complete a very special party, a host may take his guests to the theater after dinner. Be sure to arrive in plenty of time for the performance.

When taking your seat in the theater, carry it firmly with both hands. Remember to drape your tail over one arm so that it does not annoy others. Do not be afraid to ask someone to remove his or her hat if it blocks your view.

At the end of a performance, show your appreciation by clapping. Do not throw rotten vegetables; use only the *freshest* produce. Note that Skitch Farnsworth & Company prefer oily tunafish sandwiches after a good show.

It is now the host's duty to drive his guests home and see them safely to their doors.

A guest need not
feel it necessary
to invite his host
inside at this late
hour . . . except
in emergencies.

At the end of a thoroughly enjoyable evening it is correct, and indeed desirable, for both host and guest to agree, "We'll have to do it again sometime."